THE
EMPIRE STATE

A PICTURE MEMORY

Text
Bill Harris

Captions
F.M. Robertson

Design
Teddy Hartshorn

Photography
Colour Library Books Ltd
FPG International

Commissioning Editor
Andrew Preston

Editorial
David Gibbon

Production
Ruth Arthur
Sally Connolly
Andrew Whitelaw
Neil Randles

Director of Production
Gerald Hughes

CLB 2870
© 1992 Colour Library Books Ltd, Godalming, Surrey, England.
All rights reserved.
This 1992 edition published by Crescent Books,
distributed by Outlet Book Company, Inc., a Random House Company,
40 Engelhard Avenue, Avenel, New Jersey 07001.
Printed and bound in Singapore.
ISBN 0 517 07272 6
8 7 6 5 4 3 2 1

THE
EMPIRE STATE
A PICTURE MEMORY

CRESCENT BOOKS
NEW YORK • AVENEL, NEW JERSEY

Almost no one can fail to be impressed by the Hudson River Valley, but of all the people whose enthusiastic reports have come down to us through the years, Londoner Daniel Denton outdoes them all. After touring the area back in 1670, Denton wrote home that in his walks along the banks of the Hudson he never heard the least complaint of need in any of the towns and villages he passed through and noted that he was never once asked for as much as a farthing. Even the Indians were friendly, he said, and were eager to entertain strangers and to serve as guides. It was possible to sleep in the fields and woods, he claimed, "with as much security as if you were locked in your own chamber," which must have pleased the innkeepers in those friendly towns and villages. Denton also alienated a doctor or two when he noted that the valley was uncommonly healthful. "Many people in twenty years' time don't know what sickness is," he reported. "They look upon it as a great mortality if two or three die out of a town in a year's time." In his opinion, the Hudson Valley was nothing less than Canaan itself, a land whose inhabitants "are blessed with peace and plenty, blessed in their country, blessed in their fields, blessed in the fruit of their bodies, in the increase of their cattle, sheep and horses, blessed in their basket and in their store."

To which anyone interested in luring visitors to the Hudson River Valley would have to say, "Bless you, Daniel Denton." But the valley speaks for itself, and even young Denton couldn't do justice to it. It has been compared to the Rhineland and to the fjords of Norway. The Dutch were right at home there, but it filled the friends of the Duke of York with nostalgia for the English countryside. Henry James said it reminded him of the hillsides of Italy, and Henry Hudson himself expected to see the palaces of the Chinese emperors just beyond the mountains. But for all the comparing that has been done, the valley still defies comparison. Hudson probably said it best when he recorded in his log that "This is a very good land to fall in with ... and a wonderfully fine country to see."

Like most seventeenth-century explorers, Henry Hudson wasn't looking for North America, but a way around it. The Dutch controlled the sea lanes to the Orient around the tip of Africa, but they wanted to cover their bets if there was a Northwest Passage, and

they hired Hudson to sail through the Arctic, which he had done before, to see if he could find it. But once he was out at sea he turned west instead of north, to go hunting for a river his fellow Englishman, Captain John Smith, told him about. Hudson also had a map prepared eighty-five years earlier by the Italian Giovanni da Verrazano, who had sailed into the bay at the mouth of the river and noted that it was "a very pleasant situation among some steep hills."

Hudson sailed up the river as far as Cohoes, where the Mohawk empties into it, before he realized that he hadn't found the Northwest Passage, and then he headed for the open sea again. But he didn't steer his ship in the direction of Holland because he knew he'd be in trouble if he did. He had disobeyed his orders, which were quite specific that he should explore the Arctic and not the North American coast, and to add insult to injury he wound up in Cohoes instead of Cathay. The Dutch merchants weren't too pleased, and they waited a dozen years before taking possession of the river and the island at its mouth. In spite of Verrazano, whose expedition had been financed by the King of France, and the fact that a Portuguese explorer sailing in the service of Spain had long since named the river "Rio de Gomez" in his own honor, they claimed it was theirs even if they had no use for the man who had found it for them.

They pointedly refused to name the river for him and it was known as "North River" until the British drove them out in 1664 and began renaming things. The name, which still appears on nautical charts, was meant to indicate the boundary of their colony, which extended into Delaware where another line was drawn at the "South River." They didn't know that the Delaware River also ran west of them, and they also didn't know what was at the northern end of their North River. Ironically, the French had a claim there, established by Samuel de Champlain, who discovered the lake that bears his name in the same year that Hudson arrived. The two explorers were less than a hundred miles from each other, but neither of them knew it. Which was probably just as well for the relationship between France and Holland.

Neither of the explorers knew much about geology, but many years later a scientist who did said that: "The State of New York is to the geologist what the Holy

Land is to the Christian." All the major glacial formations of Eastern North America are represented within the borders of present-day New York State, and most of them are undisturbed. In many places they present a face only a geologist could love, but there are some dramatic exceptions. At the lower end of the Hudson, for instance, its west shore is marked by a wall of rock known as the Palisades. The mile-wide ridge extends from Bergen Point, near Jersey City, New Jersey, to Haverstraw, New York, about fifty miles upriver. The cliffs vary from about one-hundred feet to High Tor, an eight-hundred-foot precipice opposite Ossining. The geologists get enthused about the columnar basalt in the Palisades, which to most of us are just beautiful green rocks, and they get ecstatic about the Triassic sandstone, which adds touches of red for the pleasure of those of us who don't know the difference between the Jurassic and the Triassic periods, and possibly don't care.

Between Peekskill and Fishkill, the Hudson Highlands, rising about 1,800 feet on both sides of the river, form a twenty-mile gorge that would make the average Rhine maiden feel right at home, and beyond it, north of Newburg, the valley broadens, and off in the distance the Catskill Mountains rise nearly 4,000 feet to continue the parade of dramatic vistas, and on the east side the Berkshire Mountains of Massachusetts continue the drama.

The water is salty below Newburg, but the tides rise and fall as far up the river as Troy, some 160 miles from the sea. The tidewave through New York Bay surges up the Hudson and takes about ten hours to reach Troy, where the variation between high and low tide is about two feet, compared to Manhattan, where the difference is five-and-a-half feet.

Strictly speaking, the Hudson isn't a river like the Mohawk and others in the state. It is an arm of the sea like the fjords of Scandinavia and is technically called a "drowned river." From its source at Lake Tear of the Clouds in the Adirondacks, it flows south for 314 miles to Manhattan Island, where it disappears from view in New York Bay. But it doesn't cease to exist there. It keeps on flowing for another 580 miles past the Continental Shelf. Before the glaciers cut down the coastal mountains it flowed 330 miles further still, almost half-way to Bermuda, through what is still known as the Hudson Trough, deep under the surface of the Atlantic Ocean.

But that was long before any humans were on hand to see it. As in the rest of North America, no one knows for sure when man first arrived on the scene, but according to the written records of the Lenni-Lenape Indians, New York in general and the Hudson Valley in particular was first settled by their ancestors in about 1400, at the same time the printing press was developed in Germany and the Medicis were establishing power in Florence. The people we remember as the Delawares say that they had come from the far north in search of "The River That Flows Both Ways," and that when they found it they settled down.

The Delawares were a generally peaceful branch of the Algonquin family and, to the white man's credit, most of their land was given up by purchase rather than by force, which, except for an occasional misunderstanding, meant that life was peaceful in old New Amsterdam. But their new neighbors brought disease with them, and before the outbreak of the Revolutionary War there were no Delawares left. Part of their problem was the Iroquois, a confederation of tribes that had trouble getting along even with each other. They had joined together to protect themselves from mid-western tribes in 1570, when the great Mohawk mystic Hiawatha had a vision of five arrows tied so tightly together that they couldn't be broken. The result was what the Iroquois called "The Great Long House," a five-tribe nation that extended across the present-day State of New York. They were nothing less than bullies who managed to hound the Mohicans out of the area and into Eastern Connecticut, but they also managed to hold back the Canadian tribes along with their allies, the French, and in their way kept the English in New York and elsewhere safe from French intrusion. The English may not have taken control of Canada without them, but their loyalty to the king was their undoing when it put them on the wrong side in the Revolution.

After the war, when it was safer to go into the interior, a network of roads sprang up, not so much to get people into the west as to get the produce of their farms back to the Hudson, where it could be shipped down to New York in the fleet of sloops that had begun hauling freight and passengers on the river since the earliest days of New Amsterdam. They were reliable vessels capable of making the run from New York to Albany in about twenty-four hours. But the wind wasn't as reliable as the boats, and the trip typically took at least four days, often seven, which gave the passengers a lot of time to go ashore and do some exploring. But on August 17, 1807 the future of the Hudson Valley and the territory to the west of it was changed forever in a shower of sparks and the pungent smoke of a pinewood fire.

It was the maiden voyage of the *North River Steamboat of Clermont*. The trip from New York to Albany took thirty-two hours and the return trip was completed in thirty. Two weeks later, its inventor announced that she would carry paying passengers, at seven dollars apiece, on her second voyage. Twelve adventuresome customers took Robert Fulton up on his offer. And business improved with every trip. During the winter he increased the vessel's length by twenty feet and shortened her name to *North River*. Within five years he had built eight more steamboats and had a complete monopoly on all steam-driven shipping in New York waters.

Several men had experimented with steamboats before Robert Fulton got interested in them, but unlike them Fulton had a godfather in the person of Robert Livingston, one of the landed gentry of the Hudson Valley. He had been a law partner of John Jay, a member of the Continental Congress and a signer of the Declaration of Independence. As Chancellor of New York, it was Livingston who administered the oath of office making George Washington the first president, and later he was appointed Minister to France by Thomas Jefferson. It was there he met Fulton, a Pennsylvanian who was abroad working with the British and French governments in the development of submarines. Before leaving for home, Livingston ordered a steam engine from an English company and the grateful Fulton made Clermont, the Livingston family estate, the home port of the ship he commissioned.

Their monopoly outlived both of them, and remained until Chief Justice John Marshall ruled in 1824 that steamboats couldn't be restrained from navigating in waters open to sailboats. It shouldn't make a difference, he wrote, "if they were wafted on their voyage by the winds instead of being propelled by the agency of fire."

His decision didn't come a moment too soon. The future was at hand.

On the Fourth of July, 1817, the new Governor of New York, Dewitt Clinton, presided over the beginning of the construction of a canal that would connect the Hudson with Lake Erie and through the Great Lakes to the heartland of America. The route followed the west bank of the river to the falls at Cohoes, then cut west into the Mohawk Valley at Crescent on its way to Rome, where it headed around Lake Oneida to Syracuse. From there it went through Rochester and Lockport, where it set a course for Tonawanda and the Niagara River, before turning south and joining with the lake at Buffalo Creek. The whole project, accomplished mostly by hand, took more than eight years, during which time about the only people who weren't laughing were the Irish immigrants with the picks and shovels. Even President Jefferson said that "a canal through 350 miles of wilderness is little short of madness." But when the first flotilla of boats traveled from Buffalo to New York, with twenty-two steamboats accompanying them down the Hudson, almost no one could remember ever thinking the Erie Canal wasn't a great idea. And nearly everyone in the state could recite the statistics from memory. The canal averaged four feet deep and was twenty-eight feet wide at the bottom and forty feet at water level. It had eighty-three massive stone locks, each able to handle hundred-ton barges. Ten of them at Lockport raised and lowered the canal seventy feet. A stone aqueduct carried it over the Genesee River at Rochester, and another crossed the Mohawk River near Rexford. In many places the route was cut through solid rock and in others it went through soggy swampland. The total cost of Clinton's big ditch was about $7.6 million, but in fifty years it earned $78 million in tolls alone.

But it returned a great deal more than that. The canal made New York City the most important port on the continent, and it made the interior of New York State prosperous, fulfilling George Washington's prophecy that its farms and factories would some day be the heart of a great American Empire. It also made it possible, at a penny and a half a mile, for tourists to venture into the interior all the way up to Niagara Falls at a mile and a half an hour pace that gave them a leisurely view of the wonders of the Empire State.

But not all the wonders. Although the canal project included a sixty-acre boat basin on the shores of Brooklyn, it was as far east as the packet boats went. Anyone with a yen to see the 125 miles of ocean beach on the South Shore of Long Island had to find another way to get there. The canal skirted the wilderness of the Adirondacks, too, which may help explain why the nine-thousand square miles of virgin forest in New York's North Country is still the largest wilderness area outside of Alaska. But it wasn't as though it was hard to explore the rugged mountains by boat. There are 2,300 lakes up there, 6,000 miles of rivers and 30,000 miles of fast-moving brooks and streams. There are also 2,000 mountain peaks there, including the 5,344-ft. Mount Marcy, the source of the Hudson, which the Indians called "the cloud spitter."

Canal boat passengers also missed the Thousand Islands on the Canadian border in the St. Lawrence River. The French explorers came up with the estimate that gave them their name, but a more scientific team of surveyors subsequently put the number at 1,693 after establishing an official definition that any rock big enough to have a tree growing on it qualified as an island.

But they didn't miss New York State's most famous island, Manhattan, which owes much of its prosperity to the freight that came down the river from the Erie Canal. When Henry Hudson first passed by it was a wild, hilly place, but today the only reminder of what it looked like then is Inwood Hill at the northern tip. Most of the rest was leveled by men with picks, shovels and wheelbarrows, who not only made the terrain easier to build on, but dumped the fruit of their labor into the river and the bay, making the island bigger than Hudson would remember it. But the buildings of Manhattan notwithstanding, if their ship, the *Half Moon*, were to sail up the river today, Hudson and his crew would probably recognize many of the landmarks that haven't changed since that week in the autumn in 1609 when they took their first cruise. The view has been altered somewhat by the George Washington Bridge, the Tappan Zee Bridge and the Indian Point nuclear power plant, and they might miss Anthony's Nose, a bulbous outcropping of pink granite near Bear Mountain that was blasted away in the 1840s for a bridge that was never built. But the Storm King Mountain is still there, and it would still make them think of descriptions they'd heard of the Pacific Coast and might still make them think that China might be just beyond the horizon.

But it isn't. There is something equally facinating out there: a wonderland called New York. It always comes as a surprise to first-time visitors who think of a city, and nothing more, when they they think of New York. It's an exciting surprise, this Empire State. The city is just the beginning.

Facing page: Falaise, a French-style manor at Sands Point, built for Captain Harry F. Guggenheim in 1923.

Below: the lighthouse at Eaton's Neck Point, Long Island. Right: Sagamore Hill, the estate of President Theodore Roosevelt, and (bottom right) Coe Hall, both of which stand in Oyster Bay, Long Island. Built in 1885, Sagamore remained Roosevelt's home until his death. Coe Hall was one of the jewels of Long Island's Gold Coast when it was built in the 1920 for the insurance executive W. R. Coe. Below right: Westbury Hall, Old Westbury, which contains many beautiful English furnishings.

These pages and overleaf: New York City, the largest city in the United States and the commercial, financial and cultural center of the nation. Facing page top: the Empire State Building, completed in 1931 and, despite advances in building technology, still the third tallest building in the world. Below: the World Trade Towers, the second highest buildings on earth, which dominate Manhattan Island. The tightrope artiste Phillip Petit became famous when he walked from one tower to the other.

Above: a statue of General George S. Patton at the United States Military Academy, which he attended, at West Point (above left) on the Hudson River (overleaf). Below left: Bear Mountain State Park, the site of Bear Mountain Inn (facing page top), and (facing page bottom) Harriman State Park. Left: General Knox's headquarters at the New Windsor Cantonment, where Washington's army awaited peace at the end of the Revolution. Below: Newburgh's Minuteman statue.

The Shaker Museum (facing page, above and below) at Old Chatham comprises the country's largest collection of Shaker objects – more than 32,000 items – representing 200 years of Shaker history. There is also a museum in the Wash Room (above right) at Mount Lebanon (overleaf), where the sect's founder, Mother Ann Lee, had her base in the 1780s. She is buried in Watervliet cemetery (right). The community's well preserved Meeting House (below right) stands nearby.

Below: Albany's Empire State Plaza, where the nineteenth-century chateau-style capitol (below right and bottom right) contrasts markedly with the dramatic, futuristic 1960s designs of the office buildings nearby. The New York State Capitol took thirty years to build and cost twenty-five million dollars to construct. No expense was spared: the building boasts red granite, yellow and pink marble, stained glass, onyx and mahogany and, beside the Plaza, certainly looks colorful, flamboyant and grand.

Above, left and facing page bottom: grand buildings on Broadway in Saratoga Springs, whose mineral springs, such as Hays Spring (below), were responsible for its great popularity during the last century. Facing page top: Lincoln Baths, still the place to enjoy a soak in Saratoga Springs, and (below left) a private house near the town's Congress Park. Above left: Glens Falls, the gateway to Adirondack Park, the largest state park in the contiguous United States. Overleaf: fall in Ausable Chasm.

Above: the Champlain Monument beside Lake Champlain (facing page top) at Crown Point. Samuel de Champlain explored this area in 1609; there is also a monument to him in Plattsburgh (above right), and another there to Thomas Macdonough (below right) who defeated the British in 1814. In nearby Ticonderoga are the Liberty Monument (right) and Fort Ticonderoga (facing page bottom). Below: near Route 86 near the Whiteface Mountains, and (overleaf) Ausable Chasm.

Lake Placid (above left and below) is one of the most famous year-round vacation centers in the East, claiming the Intervale Olympic Ski Jump complex, specially constructed for the 1980 Winter Olympic games and since open to the public. Facing page: (bottom) Mirror Lake, Lake Placid, and (above) Long Lake to its south. Left: the John Brown Historic Site, the last home of the abolitionist, and (above) High Falls Gorge in Wilmington. Below left: White Lake in Adirondack Park.

Facing page top: the summit of Whiteface Mountain near Wilmington. The solitary peak is 4,867 feet high and its twenty-eight trails (overleaf) are besieged by skiers in the winter, while in warmer months many simply drive up the slopes to admire the famous panoramic view (facing page bottom), which includes Lake Placid. Below: the Ausable River in the fall. This waterway flows at the base of Whiteface Mountain, forming the High Falls Gorge before it drains into Lake Champlain via Ausable Chasm.

Below: Boldt Castle on Heart Island in the St. Lawrence River. The castle was built by a German immigrant, George C. Boldt, who worked his way up in the hotel industry from dishwasher to the owner of the Waldorf-Astoria. The castle, built as a present for his wife, was never finished, since she died during its construction. Right: one of the islands in the Thousand Islands, (below right) the Oswegatchie River, and (bottom right) an outdoor café in Alexandria Bay on the St. Lawrence Seaway.

Cooperstown was founded in 1786 by Judge William Cooper, the father of James Fenimore Cooper, author of the classic The Last of the Mohicans. *Facing page top: Fenimore House, a museum exhibiting Cooper memorabilia, and (above, above left, left and below left) the National Baseball Hall of Fame and Museum, where the history of baseball and its heroes are celebrated, both in Cooperstown. Facing page bottom: Cooperstown Farmers' Museum, and (below) Binghampton.*

51

Below right: McGraw Hall in Cornell University, Ithaca. Established in 1865, the university was unusual for its time, since it was co-educational and non-sectarian. Remaining pictures: Syracuse, which was a prosperous industrial town well before it was reached by the Erie Canal in the late 1820s, though this waterway did increase the city's share of trade. Syracuse University (right and bottom right) started in 1870 with forty-one students; today 16,000 are enrolled in this major institution.

Below: Taughannock Falls, a state recreation area north of Ithaca, and (overleaf) Montour Falls, a town near Watkins Glen. Both destinations lie in the Finger Lakes Region (facing page top) in the west of the state, an historic area, once full of game, that originally belonged to the Five Nations of the Iroquois Indians. Lake Seneca (facing page bottom) is the deepest of these eleven long, thin stretches of water, reaching a depth of 630 feet, while Lake Cayuga is the longest, at forty miles.

Facing page: Rochester, home of George Eastman, the inventor of the Kodak camera, who simplified photography sufficiently to put it within the reach of the masses and made a fortune as a result. The George Eastman House (below) was built by the millionaire and left to the University of Rochester in 1932. It has been expanded to include the International Museum of Photography. Above: Old Fort Niagara, Youngstown, (above right) Olcott marina, and (below right) Braddock Bay state marina. Right: spick and span Rochester Coast Guard station.

Buffalo (these pages) is the state's second largest city. Above: the Soldiers and Sailors monument on Lafayette Square, and (above left) Naval and Servicemen's Park on the Buffalo River, which contains a fascinating collection of World War II military equipment. Left: Kern Street, (below) Buffalo's majestic Town Hall, and (below left) Forest Lawn Cemetery. Overleaf and following page: the American Falls, which, with Luna and Horseshoe Falls, are all referred to as Niagara Falls.